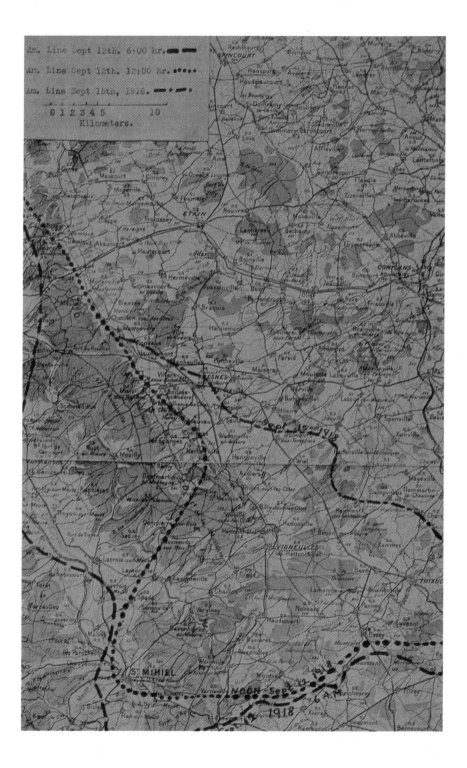

Am. Line Sept 12th. 6:00 hr.
Am. Line Sept 12th. 12:00 hr.
Am. Line Sept 16th, 1918.

```
0 1 2 3 4 5          10
        Kilometers.
```

The Lion Killers

BILLY MITCHELL AND THE BIRTH OF STRATEGIC BOMBING
— SECOND EDITION —

The publication of this book would not have been possible without the aid of the following
sources. We would like to thank the Library of Congress, Manuscript Reading Room; the
National Archives, Still-Photography Division, College Park; the Graveyard of the Atlantic
Museum; and the Hatteras Island Genealogical and Historical Society. Special Thanks to Joseph
and Melanie Schwarzer, Dale Burrus, Natalie Perry, Mel Covey, Ricky Jones, Josephine Oden,
Carlos Oden, Ray and BJ Midgett, Ronald Stowe, Kevin Duffus, George and Sylvia Taylor,
Gary Austin and family, Drew Pullen, Debra Rezeli, and Bob Drapala.

For any questions or comments, you can reach the author at 252-995-6956.

Published by Aerial Perspective
428 Cripps Drive
Mt. Holly, New Jersey 08060

ISBN 0-9748602-0-4

Second Printing

Printed in United States of America

The Lion Killers

BILLY MITCHELL AND THE BIRTH OF STRATEGIC BOMBING
— SECOND EDITION —

Written by William Schwarzer
Photographic Reproduction by Robert V. Drapala
Design by Debra D. Rezeli

Introduction

This is a story about the birth of air power. It is about people who loved their country and fought to keep its ideals alive. One such man was William Mitchell. A staunch advocate of air power, Mitchell's ideas were controversial in a time when the General and the Admiral were deemed the sole proprietors of modern warfare. It was a time when one of the most important events in the development of national defense took place, an event that is scarcely known today.

Although much has been written about the trials faced by America's first military aircraft, little if anything has been published specifically recounting the events that occurred on Hatteras Island, North Carolina. The bombing test that took place off the Outer Banks in 1923 proved conclusively the strength and future of air power.

History is the passing of memories from one generation to another. This is a history uniquely American. It includes the faces and stories of a small coastal community, of world leaders, and of the man who brought them together.

Every human birth engenders the possibility that history will take a new and better course. Those born with the perception to realize what most see as impossible, experience the blessing and the curse of a visionary. It was so with Mitchell all his life. His military career took him to the jungles of Cuba and the Philippines, the snowy wilderness of Alaska, the battlefields of Europe and the political battleground of Washington, DC. A prophet in some respects, he predicted the attacks on Pearl Harbor and New York City decades before they occurred. He was the first to realize the full military potential of aircraft prior to the Second World War. Mitchell's many articles, speeches, and his historic bombing trials eventually proved the need for an air force. Ironically, it was this same outspoken personality that led to his court martial in 1926. His theories were never fully appreciated until the later half of the 20th century.

Today, to those who do know of him, Mitchell is still a controversial figure. To some, he is the heroic lone patriot fighting against bureaucracy and military politics for the good of national security. To others, Mitchell is nothing more than an egotistical charlatan, more interested in grand standing than the future of air power. Regardless, William Mitchell, above all, was a true American hero. He was a visionary in a complex time, a soldier dedicated to his country, and a brilliant strategist.

Only through the perspective of history can true achievement be recognized. A single life can be made up of a thousand memories, and sometimes one defining event which changes everything. Like most stories this begins with birth, ends with death and somewhere in between gives us a model of how to carry on in the face of adversity. Between the lines of genius and fanaticism lies the shade of gray that continues to keep great minds a secret. This is a story of achievement and a life that demanded the incredible; this is the story of William Mitchell.

Chapter One
"...We were regulars..."

During their vacation in southern France on December 29th, 1879, Harriet Danforth Becker and John Lendrum Mitchell became parents of a baby boy. William Mitchell was the first of four children: one brother, John and three sisters; Harriet, Janet and Ruth. Mitchell's father was a Senator from Wisconsin and the patriarch of what had become a family dynasty in Milwaukee. At age twelve, William Mitchell attended Racine College, an Episcopal preparatory school for young men. Leaving home for the first time, he began a life long routine of writing to his parents. In a letter dated the 23rd of May 1894, Mitchell wrote his father, reporting on his academic performance and plans for further schooling after graduation.

> *...I do not think I will pass in rhetoric this year however. (sic)I have enough English to get into college now. The catalogue of the Columbian University of Washington says that "candidates for admission to any class of the college must, unless that (sic) are graduates of the preparatory school or of the high schools of Washington, sustain an examination in the following...I am going to take the part of a girl in our play. Will you buy some tickets? Don't tell mamma which part I take or that I am in it. I am going to get some pictures taken + I wish to see if she will know me.*

A great number of his letters often requested money for everything from train tickets to sporting equipment and, coming from a wealthy political family, Mitchell was often indulged as a child. However, there were aspects of his personality that were constantly seeking the approval and, most importantly, the attention of his parents. His love of Washington and wish to be close to his family influenced his interest in Colombian, now George Washington, University. He entered Colombian University in 1895 at age sixteen. He was the youngest student enrolled. Contrary to Mitchell's decent academic performance at Racine his grades slowly began to deteriorate at Colombian. Sports took a priority. He had a competitive and adventurous spirit and dreams of glory fueled throughout his childhood by heroic tales of the Civil War. Three years later, his dreams came true. It was a year that would have an effect on the rest of Mitchell's life; the year he began his military career.

In Spring, 1898 the tiny island of Cuba became the focus and rallying point of a nation's attention and pride. Prior to 1898, the United States had invested at least fifty million dollars in the Cuban sugar trade. The return averaged a hundred million dollars a year. With the threat of Spanish colonization, the growing sentiment in the US was anti-Spanish and pro a free, independent Cuba. However, on the evening of February 15th, an explosion set off the powder magazine on the battleship *USS Maine*, causing the tragic destruction and subsequent sinking of the ship. Two hundred and sixty American sailors were killed instantly. A passionate media, run by politicians eager for war, quickly labeled the 'attack' on the *Maine* as the responsibility of the Spanish government. Two months later, America officially declared war on Spain. United purpose against a common enemy gave hope to a country still healing from civil war. Again, a generation answered the call to their nation's service.

Fathers, who have fought in war, dread their sons will leave home to do the same. Senator John Mitchell was no exception. William Mitchell was graduated early from Colombian to join the 1st Wisconsin Volunteer Infantry Regiment. Regardless of John Mitchell's disapproval of his son leaving college early to join the Army, he would not stand in the way of his choice. With the help of his father, Mitchell was commissioned a second Lieutenant in company M. Like so many other young men of his generation, he was caught up in the illusion of war being a great adventure:

Signal Corps, Camp Jacksonville

Our way to Tampa about 100 miles south of Nashville Tenn.

Saturday May 21 - 1898

My Dear Mother

My time has been so taken up since I joined the army that I have hardly had time to do anything. I only went to town twice while at Cau ... We have a fine regiment the 1st + the 2nd +3 are nearly as good they are at Chic... park now. They are a strapping big lot of fellows are on the average nearly as tall as I and much heavier. We have had awful weather at Camp Harvey since the day we encamped. As I write people are cheering, flags are waving and bands playing all along the road are continued good bye. There were some pretty touching farewells paid when the boys left with women fainting + crying all around like the world was coming to an end. We got off the train at Nashville to get some exercise + marched a few miles. Everyone thought us regulars on account of our equipment + fine drilling. We were regulars now...

Optimism and naiveté concerning late 19th century warfare were characteristic of Mitchell's letters home. In one letter, after describing his frustrations of not being sent into combat, he requested his mother send him a gold helmet braid as there were none to be found where he was stationed. His eagerness to see action in Cuba was only surpassed by his boldness towards superiors in requesting to be deployed as soon as possible. Shortly after arriving in Florida, Mitchell was detached from the 1st Wisconsin and ordered to accept a commission in the Signal Corps. In later years he would comment:

> I knew little about what this meant and did not relish leaving my organization, as we expected to be fighting the Spaniards in Cuba in a short time. However, orders were orders, and I was assigned as a second Lieutenant to the 2nd Volunteer Signal Corp…

After receiving training as a signal officer in Washington, Mitchell was assigned under General Greely, and left for Camp Cuba Libre in Jacksonville. The desire to fight the Spanish imperialists, who he referred to as 'bandits', was greater than ever.

> Camp Cuba Libre, September 21st 98
>
> My Dear Mother,
>
> I have just written a letter to Colonel Dunwoody telling him about my desire of going to Cuba. Father wrote that he saw the Colonel the other day and the Colonel asked him if I wanted to go to Cuba. So I have written him so as to have it fully understood. I don't want him to assign me to this company if it is going to be mustered out.

In the same letter, Mitchell describes the effects various diseases were having on the Wisconsin regiment. Typhoid was running rampant through Camp Cuba Libre. The physicians on call often mistook it as malaria; a misdiagnosis that accounted for the unusually high mortality rate. Mitchell became more and more distraught as days turned into weeks and weeks into months. Neither he nor his regiment were headed to Cuba. A letter to his mother indicates the conditions and his conduct at Camp Cuba Libre.

Second Lieutenant Mitchell (far left) posing with staff members of the Signal Corps

There is no use in the world to be writing about getting sick, sick, sick. The first thing you know probably now I will be home... I am very much disgusted affairs have taken this turn but I suppose that is for the greater good. The weather here is simply delightful and I am feeling better, I weigh more than I ever did before. ...today we have nearly three hundred cases (of typhoid) in this division hospital here...I have never been sick in camp yet ...We had a squadron review yesterday and the commanding officer commended me for my work before the other officers and he is...old regular army now.

Mitchell's physical condition spared him from the onslaught of disease. Consequently, he often did duty for others in his company who were ill. He became an example of steadfastness and leadership to his men, and his superiors noted this. However, typhoid had taken a heavy toll on the 1st Wisconsin, and in September forced the majority of the regiment to be mustered out. Mitchell, assigned to the Signal Corps, was still active in the Army, and now sought any way possible to get to Cuba.

...If it comes down to a recommendation now Col. Maxfield we will get it sure because he thinks that we have the finest Company in the

Signal Corp...I am going to try to get on some Brigade or Corps staff...If I can not do that I am sure I think to get a place in the line, and if they are going to send any Volunteer Cavalry to Cuba would like to get into that. ...of course I should rather stay in the signal corps than any other branch but wish to stay in the army too a year anyway if I want to get over to Cuba."

In December 1898, Mitchell got his wish. He and his company under an order by Col. Dunwoody, chief signal officer, were to establish a network of telegraph lines in the Santiago province of Cuba. Being exposed to a war torn, disease-ridden Cuba crippled by ongoing conflict, had a profound effect on Mitchell. He emerged from the jungle; the naiveté gone, yet the optimism remained, creating a responsible leader with a seemingly unconquerable spirit.

Regardless of his experiences in Cuba, Mitchell's thirst for adventure persisted. With the outbreak of the Philippine Insurrection, on February 4th 1899, Mitchell, once more, desperately tried to get a transfer from his current deployment in the Santiago province to an active theater of operations. He wrote to his father expressing his frustration.

...Here I have been since the war without any foreign service to speak of and have not been in any engagements as of yet. How would you have felt in the Civil War if you had been out of the way somewhere?

After two weeks, Mitchell was given a reassignment to the Philippines. The limited challenges of Cuba would barely be a dress rehearsal for his new post. Packs of wild dogs, roving units of *insurrectos*, and America's first experiences with jungle warfare served as a rude awakening to Mitchell's curiosity, but one he tackled with as much ferocity as he had his previous difficulties. The conflict in the Philippines would last until 1901 and, by its end, make a war weary veteran of Mitchell. During those years, he also traveled to Europe, explored Asia, and briefly operated as an army intelligence officer in Manchuria. At the start of a new century, Mitchell would find himself on another adventure in the icy climate of Alaska. Still

Mitchell (right) in the Philippines

assigned to the Signal Corps, Mitchell was laying telegraph line through the American arctic frontier. It was at this time he began a love affair with something that would last all his life; his love of flight. While stationed at Skagway, Mitchell taught himself the basics of aerodynamics.

> *Even while engaged in the construction of telegraph lines in arctic Alaska, I was studying assiduously the development and handling of lighter-than-air craft, kites and gliders, and it served me in good stead, not only when I first took up aviation in earnest…*

Mitchell would leave Alaska with the rank of Captain, and, in 1903, married his first wife, Caroline Stoddard. Regardless of how youthful or intemperate Mitchell may have seemed in his early years as a soldier, his experiences, thus far, were becoming the stuff of legend. His journey began, as it would end, in the midst of a private war and a world on the edge of conflict.

Capt. Mitchell atop signal tower

Mitchell in Alaska

Chapter Two
"...The Sky Would Be Black..."

*I*n 1914, a Serbian nationalist named Gavrilo Princip was watching the Archduke Franz Ferdinand and Duchess Sophie von Chotkova walk to their carriage behind City Hall in Sarajevo. In a span of two minutes, history would be changed forever. Princip's assassination of the Archduke and the Duchess set off a domino effect in the European alliances that quickly fomented dissension between the super powers of the old world. This single act of terror rekindled old hatreds and time worn prejudices. Within a heartbeat, half of the world was at war. French cuirassiers charged German machine gun emplacements, Saudi tribesman armed with swords and flintlock rifles were butchered by Turkish artillery. It was the end of an era and the birth of a modern age. Throughout this period, the weapons to wage a new kind of war were developed. Of these weapons, the emergence of air power was the most profound change to arise from a conflict in which the use of horse mounted cavalry was common. However, as nations fought for their existence, the United States was doing its best to stay out of the conflict all together. The nation teetered between extremist doctrines that ran from pacifism to a militaristic manifest destiny during much of the First World War. In the midst of confusion, one man attempted to prepare an army for the inevitable.

In 1917, William Mitchell, a Major in the aviation section of the Signal Corps, secured a position as an observer in France during the Spring of that year. Long standing neutrality in the United States had weakened. Growing numbers of English and French sympathizers, along with incidents like the sinking of the *Lusitania,* hardened views against Imperial

Propeller used as a grave marker for an allied pilot.

Artillery in front of St. Mihiel

Germany. Unrestricted U-boat warfare against American shipping result-ed in the end of diplomatic relations with Germany. Only a few months later, and only a week after Mitchell's arrival in France, America was at war. The controversial Zimmerman telegram, proposing Mexico ally with Germany in the event the United States no longer remained neutral, incited public outrage and lead President Wilson to seek Congressional approval for a Declaration of War. Upon Mitchell's arrival in Paris, he launched himself into the fray. He tried to gather any and all information that would be helpful to the US Army. Patriotic Americans back home read a news article published in June, reporting Mitchell's activities overseas a month before his promotion to Lieutenant Colonel.

An American army aviator has been in active service, flying over German lines at Verdun and elsewhere during the past week. He is Major William Mitchell of the aviation section of the Signal Corp. The announcement was made at American army headquarters today. ...He has the distinction of being the first American regular army officer to "get into action" on the western front in the air. Presumably he acted as observer, with a French army officer as pilot. Major William Mitchell...is an air pioneer

Mitchell was a pioneer in every sense. The following is a series of excerpts from Mitchell's journal regarding his observations of the latest tactics, camouflage, and technology being implemented by both sides during the last three years of war. There is irony in the fact that the listening equipment being engineered on the battlefields of France, was a primitive ancestor to the kind of aircraft early warning system used by the RAF with great success during the Battle of Britain decades later.

...I neglected to mention that I had visited a listening post for aircraft earlier in the day. This was equipped with a listener which consisted of several megraphones(sic) grouped in the same frame with a diaphragm and ear pieces like a stethoscope. Very minute sounds can be heard with it. A whisper can be heard for several hundred feet; the noise of the town in the distance was very plain. With it were the ordinary telescopes and optical instruments used by artillery for observation, a 60-inch searchlight with its automobile generator etc. always ready to begin and anti-aircraft guns along side. The whole outfit was on a commanding position on a hill back of the town. The men in charge said that the listener was pretty good but by no means

Mitchell in World War I

Eddie Rickenbaker poses beside Spad XIII of the 94th Aero Squadron

anything remarkable as it reproduced all sounds and sometimes it was difficult to tell which was which. ...

... There is another detector used, said to be employed by the Germans. This is a very delicately balanced gold door in circuit with an electro magnet which records time when the circuit is broken. This is placed over an orifice in the top of a large barrel. The door is about one half inch square and the orifice in the barrel is a pipe about three inches in diameter brought to a small opening just under the door. When the sound wave hits the barrel, the door opens and breaks the circuit; this makes a clock record the time; the same thing happens at the other barrel of the station. The rest is the same as for the other system. This is thought to be very good. ...

... The batteries were all camouflaged, that is hidden by artificial means, the guns themselves were painted with blotched colors, while over them all was the grass matting of the camouflage colors. Everything is concealed in the best way possible. It is much harder to conceal from the observation of aircraft than from the ground. ...

Mitchell in cockpit of Thomas Morse Scout pursuit plane

... For attack the company is formed in two echelons of two ranks each. The first echelon has men deployed on a 3 yard interval, the individual machine gun men and rifle grenade men are in the first rank, the ammunition carries and hand grenadiers are in the second rank deployed on the same interval about ten yards to the rear. Behind these a couple of squads "cleaners of trenches" follow. These are armed with pistols, knives, etc., and carry (sic)sulphur bombs to throw into the abris, of the enemy to make them come out. They have "flamenwerfers" and anything necessary for close combat. ...

Despite Mitchell's extremely detailed reports regarding what had been the most effective means of combat from 1914-1917, Washington ignored his plans for an American Air Corps. Numerous requests for office expenses, equipment and personnel for the development of the aviation wing of the Army were either regarded as unnecessary or simply not considered. The problem of funding was not exclusively Mitchell's, as aviation expenses for the American Expeditionary Forces (AEF) were also difficult for General Pershing to obtain. Running out of time, Major Mitchell personally began

World War I trench

an aviation office in France with his own money and contributions from *"patriotic French and Americans in the service"* as well as financial aid from private citizens in the states. Le Bourget Airdrome was one of the first schools used to train American pilots to fly in combat. Among the many airmen trained at Le Bourget, was a famous race car driver from the United States named Eddie Rickenbacker. After Mitchell's car had broken down on the side of the road, he met Rickenbacker who was then a mechanic and had expressed interest in the Air Service. Eddie Rickenbacker would go on to become one of America's first war aces. This was the birth of the Army Air Corps in First World War.

In a diary entry written on the 29th of April, Mitchell describes his first air raid.

> *When we had finished dinner at the little mess it was dark and a beautiful moon had arisen ? full. We remarked that it was a good night for a bombing and we knew that the French bombers were to start on their errands themselves. I went back to the hotel to write up the occurrences of the day. As I was writing I heard the hum of a*

Mitchell conversing with allied officers

Mitchell's DeHavilland DH-4B with command pennant on rudder

strange motor and almost immediately Zing-zing-zing and then all the windows and doors shook. They were very very heavy explosions and seemed quite near. I looked at my watch, it was just a quarter to 11 p.m. Search lights were immediately turned on the sky. The hum of many motors then became very plain and the anti-aircraft guns opened. Another series of strong explosions, then the machine gun and anti-aircraft fire. The whole town was, of course, in darkness and everyone had taken to the vaces or vaulted wine cellars inside of the houses.

He was starting to see the possibilities of strategic bombing and its effects on supply lines, troop movements and morale. Washington bureaucrats continued to ignore the course warfare was taking and funds had yet to arrive to support Mitchell's growing air armada. A month after the raid, he arrived at the Chateau Roux, and was subsequently placed in charge of American air operations.

July 1917

On July 12th, 1917 I flew from the Le Bourget Airdrome, near Paris, to

Mitchell in flight suit beside DH-4

Mitchell inspecting plane

Mitchell at award ceremony for airmen

the Chateau Roux, France, in an 18 meter Nieuport airplane, a distance of 156 miles each way, or 312 miles for the round trip. It took 5 hrs. 45 minutes. I, of course, was alone on this trip and it was the first long distance flight of this kind I had made. The French were quite astonished that anybody could fly that far across France without knowing it and never having been in that part of the country before.

On July 13th I found myself in charge of all aviation arrangement in Europe and with only six (6) American officers under me fit for duty. This was more than three months after the war had been declared. As we could get nothing definite from the United States in answer to our cablegrams and letters, it was evident that we would have to organize our own forces from what we could get hold of in Europe.

Mitchell's experience was not limited to the skies over France. He ventured to the front often and came under enemy fire numerous times. At one time, he was in a bunker when it received simultaneous hits from a pair of nine-inch shells.

As the American air war began in Europe, so did the losses of American soldiers in combat. Though Mitchell, now a Colonel, would survive, he was not untouched by the carnage. His younger brother, John

Courtesy of National Archives, Maryland

Mitchell with command staff

Mitchell, was killed in the summer of 1918 while trying to land a severely damaged plane. William wrote to his sister Ruth, describing his feelings.

> To begin with he was my only brother he was so much younger that he was like a son, and he was the ? as a great friend. He had every quality that I wanted in a brother and admired in a man. I suppose he was very nearly the dearest living thing in the world to me. There is little use talking about it because it is all over.

John's death was something Mitchell would never forget and he would always feel responsible. The air war in the skies over France was raging and American pilots were now fighting in the thick of it. Mitchell undaunted by personal tragedy, continued to lead his men.

> On July 16 we counterattacked the Germans opposite the left flank of the Fifth French Army. Zero hour was at 12 noon, and our whole aviation participated in it. We had some violent combat; just held our own in fine shape. We attack in echelon by flights of five airplanes each, one after the other. The Germans fly in a group of about five airplanes-a fan formation, as they call it, which, when it hits one of our flights, spreads out on both flanks and attempts to get over, under, and on each side of it.

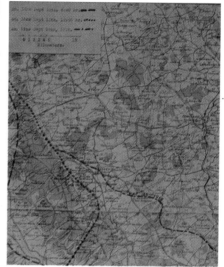

Mitchell visits airdrome

Map of St. Mihiel salient

Over the past few months, Germany had been bled white trying to regain a strategic advantage for an offensive. America's involvement was taking its toll and bringing swift resolution to the conflict on the wings of allied aviators. Mitchell wrote home to his mother detailing the sheer magnitude of air operations.

> *Dear Mummy,*
>
> *I am in a new field of activity and command all American, French and British air troops and services in our area. Some day I shall write and tell you about the number of airplanes. Should they fly at once the sky would be black.*

Both sides were growing exhausted from heavy losses during the last four years, and the war was slowly drawing to a close.

Since the Marne Offensive of 1918, plans had been formulated to deal a crushing counterattack that would break the back of the German lines. Mitchell describes the beginning of what would become known as the battle for St. Mihiel in his diary.

> *The shape of the front-that is, the St. Mihiel salient-furnishes an interesting situation. It projects into our line in the shape of a horseshoe,*

rather sharp one at the toe to be sure. This point of the toe is located at the city of St. Mihiel. The Germans pushed in here in 1915 and occupied it in an attempt to isolate Verdun and surround it so as to cause its surrender.

It must be remembered that the most direct line of advance from Germany into France is through Coblenz, Treves, Verdun, Nancy, and then straight towards Lyons where the centers of population and factories of France are located.

…September 12th had been decided upon as the day of our grand attack. It was the greatest army ever assembled under the American flag-400,000 men with about 3,000 cannon facing the enemy. Our air force consisted of nearly 1,500 airplanes.

To attain a road into Germany and victory, the St. Mihiel salient had to be taken. The Germans knew they could not hold the city. However, if the allied troops could be delayed long enough, it would buy time for a new counter offensive. Precious time was lost as German soldiers fell back, retreated out of the town and found better positions. It presented a unique opportunity for the allies to bring a swift conclusion to the war.

During a staff meeting with General Pershing, the Army chief engineer recommended the attack be delayed on the grounds that weather conditions would prevent supplies such as water and ammunition from reaching the advancing troops. Colonel Mitchell was present at the meeting and, although he was the most junior officer on the staff, he convinced Pershing the offensive could not be postponed.

The Germans were withdrawing from St. Mihiel…our troops were now in position for the attack…all we had to do was to jump on the Germans, and the quicker we did it, the better.

General Pershing smiled and ordered the attack.

Mitchell had the long awaited opportunity to prove that air power could be used as an effective tool for close support of infantry. He took command of the largest air service ever assembled under one command to that date.

CAPTURING ST. MIHIEL SALIENT
This photograph graphically shows the speed with which the American artillerymen worked. A shell case flying through the air and a new shell sliding into the breech in the same fraction of a second.

My Dear Mummy,

My dear mummy. Just a note to let you know that I am well and at this moment I have directly under my command the largest aviation service brought under one command on this front. I shall write you sometime of the number of ships etc....

Heavy preparation went into coordinating the ground and air elements the day before the attack. The pilots and crews were given their targets, the infantryman moved into position, and the allies gathered strength for one of the last great battles of the First World War. Mitchell described the start of the advance, including the actions of a young George Patton.

The morning of September 12th dawned dark and cloudy, with intermittent rain. Clouds hung low and the visibility was very poor. Nevertheless, our Air Service, with that of our allies went over the lines, and I was much pleased with the fact that virtually no German

CAPTURING ST. MIHIEL SALIENT.
Stone dugout entrance built by the Germans in 1914 on the side of a hill. The first Americans to explore the hill after its capture found that an underground passage led from there to an observation point on the crest of the height.

airplanes got over our ground troops. We forced the German airmen to fight away back of Vigneulles and Conflans, thirty miles away from our ground troops. We had many combats at these places during the day. On September 13th we could see that the enemy was concentrating all his available air power against us because he was loosing too many prisoners and equipment. Our air force, however, by attacking their transportation trains, railroads, and columns on the roads, piled them up with debris so that it was impossible for many of their troops to get away quickly, resulting in their capture by our infantry. …The Battle of St. Mihiel was really over on the first day, and every objective had been accomplished. I was glad to see that our tanks did so well because I am convinced that in the future the tank will be the only means of advancing on the ground against a well intrenched (sic) and determined enemy. George Patten (sic) rode into St. Mihiel on the back of one of these tanks away ahead of any other ground troops in the vicinity. This is the kind of stuff we need.

CAPTURING ST. MIHIEL SALIENT.
In a town in the heart of the St. Mihiel salient the victorious American troops took time to change one of the German street signs from "Hidenburg Strasse" to " Wilson, U.S.A." A glimpse of the brief and informal ceremony.

By September 16th, the St. Mihiel salient was completely captured and occupied by the allies. American military might had become a formidable machine and the capture of St. Mihiel was a symbol of that accomplishment. General Pershing wrote Colonel Mitchell, congratulating him on role the air service had in the victory:

My Dear Colonel,

Please accept my sincere congratulations on the successful and very important part taken by the Air forces under your command in the first offensive of the First American Army. The organization and control of the tremendous concentration of Air forces, including American, French, British, and Italian units, which had enabled the Air Service of the First Army to carry out so successfully its dangerous and important mission, is as fine a tribute to you personally as is the courage and nerve shown by your officers a signal proof of the high moral which permeates the service under your command.

General Pershing (front row, right of center) posing with group of allied commanders.

Please convey to your command my heartfelt appreciation of their work. I am proud of you all.

Sincerely yours,

JOHN J. PERSHING.

Eight days later, Mitchell, now promoted to Brigadier General, began another series of bombings against the enemy front and remaining supply lines. His plans for continuing the air war were brought to an end with the beginning of peace negotiations at Versailles.

Few were aware of how best to implement air power as a new weapon. More importantly, fewer had any idea of how to control it within the Army. From 1917 to 1919, there were three different positions that held the title of Chief of the Air Service. In November 1917, General Benjamin Foulois was made Chief of the Air Service for the AEF. Foulois was the very first Army aviator, and had learned to fly on the Army's first aircraft, the Wright 1909 Flyer. He was also the chairman of the Joint Army and Navy Technical Aircraft Committee of the War and Navy Departments with responsibility for production, organization, maintenance and operations of all American aeronautical material and

BRIG. GEN. WILLIAM MITCHELL, CHIEF OF AIR SERVICE AND STAFF.
Left to right : Capt. R. Rallois; Lieut. Col. L.H. Brereton; Brig. Gen William Mitchell; Maj. Ira Cobaleman; Capt. O.F. Marre; 1st Lieut. EP. Schwab. Dierder, Germany.

personnel throughout Europe. These were responsibilities Foulois would retrain even after being appointed Chief of Air Service, AEF. Foulois was Chief of Air Service while Mitchell was trying to get funding and material for the Army air wing. Mitchell and Foulois often disagreed and worked at cross-purposes. Foulois's life had eerily paralleled Mitchell's. They were born the same year, both served in the Spanish American War and Philippines, both had been on the cutting edge of history in the development of powered flight, and both would find themselves fighting for the preservation of air power at different times in their careers. Mitchell was Chief of Air Service, Army Group and commanded all Air Service units on the Front. He would be appointed assistant Chief of the Air Service in 1919. Thomas Milling was Chief of Air Service for the First Army and chief of Mitchell's general staff. Major General Mason Patrick replaced Foulois as Chief of Air Service, AEF in May of 1918. Ironically, Patrick was not a supporter of air power. Mitchell's fate, as well as Foulois's, would be intertwined with Patrick over the next decade.

Mitchell beside captured Fokker DVII

Mitchell's experiences in Europe fueled his ambitions for the creation of a separate Air Service outside of the Army. He believed that, after proving itself time and again, the future of military aviation was assured.

Although he had survived one of the most traumatic conflicts in human history, Mitchell's difficulties were just beginning. Ironically, the war for control of the air would not be fought in Europe, but in Washington.

Chapter Three

"This Could Happen–It May Happen"

*A*s the United States entered the roaring twenties, carefree days and nights became the concern of a public desperate to forget the dark days of World War One.

As the world returned to peace, the controversy over air power was heating up. Aviation became a political football in the midst of a very public revaluation of the nation's defense. Congress formed committees to explore the future of the Air Service all to little or no avail. With the end of the war to end all wars, many asked the question; why do we need a military? In the midst of a recession, air power was toted as an economic alternative to million dollar battleships. Other branches of the military began to panic; afraid of loosing even more funding.

It is a fact of history that the worst tragedies are often repeated. As before, people had reached complacency through an illusion of security and prosperity. This, when combined with a failure of imagination, results in the repetition of historical tragedy. As popular support for an Air Service separate from the Army and Navy grew, conflicts arose among politicians and military officials who had little knowledge of aviation.

Admiral William Benson, the first Chief of Naval Operations, severely reduced the naval air wing and instigated a more pronounced debate between the Navy and the Air Service. In the midst of this was Brigadier General William 'Billy' Mitchell who had become a public icon for American aviation. Mitchell was resolute in his beliefs that a need for a separate Aviation Department was a necessity. Over the months of hearings and private ridicule of Mitchell's ideas, President Harding promised to create

Courtesy of Library of Congress

a separate Air Force if airplanes could sink warships. The Washington Star reported the scheduling of the first tests on March 23rd 1921.

> *He challenged the Navy to provide a ship that his flying men could sink. This brought a laugh from the former Secretary of the Navy Daniels and jests from naval officers, but congress took the suggestion seriously. …And so the demonstration is to take place as summer*

Mitchell at an air race

Mitchell (right) speaking with allied Major General Mason Patrick

opens at a point probably not far from Cape Hatteras, although details of the arrangement are being held back by the censor.

Mitchell's outspoken manner before congress and his assessment of the battleship as being obsolete attracted the attention of the media and ensured his controversial legacy. Even those who had been allies at first were

Mitchell (right) in front of DH-4   Mitchell with airmen

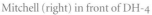

desperate to be rid of an egotistical upstart, whom the media had nick-
named 'Petrel'. Mitchell had written a report earlier that year outlining the
vulnerability of a Naval station in Hawaii called Pearl Harbor, and how it
could be easily threatened by an air attack. His report of the hypothetical
attack was so accurate, it differed only by twenty minutes in the timing of
the actual attack in 1941. Since the end of the war, Mitchell had continually
drawn attention toward the increasing inadequacy of the nation's defenses.
The treaty of Versailles had ensured another world war. Many understood
the harsh restrictions on Germany would create profound resentment that
would boil over within the next two decades. Nevertheless, few wished to
face the reality. Mitchell understood the nation needed to prepare for the
inevitable. He did not suffer from a lack of imagination or logical thought.
However, this, combined with his sincere concern for and fervent dedica-
tion to the country, often resulted in tactless conduct. An article written in
the New York Sun in June 1921, describes a dispute between Mitchell and
General Charles T. Menoher, regarding the Brigadier General's use of an air
disaster as justification for a separate Air Service.

> *Relief of Brig-Gen. William Mitchell as assistant Chief of the United*
> *States Army air service has been requested by his chief, Major-Gen.*

Mitchell (left), Orville Wright (center), Admiral W. F. Fullam (right) at an air race.

Charles T. Menoher, in a formal communication to the Secretary of War Weeks. While secretary Weeks did not say directly what action he would take, he indicated that all the precedents of army discipline and service would probably cause him to accede to the request and assign some one else to the position…Menoher's request is a direct result of a statement issued by Mitchell after the disastrous fall of the Eagle airplane on May 28th which resulted in the death of seven lives. Mitchell used this disaster as a text for a plea for a unified air service and in doing so ran counter to the sentiments and desires of his chief, who did not believe that propaganda for a unified service should have been put out by Mitchell. …the air service, a thing that has become distasteful to Menoher and which he construes as having undermined the morale of his command.

Disagreements would continue to arise between Mitchell and Menoher, usually due to Mitchell's overly independent command of the Air Service, and his lack of regard for the chain of command. The son of a politician was hardly a diplomat. The air trials, originally scheduled to take place off Cape Hatteras, North Carolina were moved to the Virginia Capes. Mitchell trained

Pilots training for the bombing trials, possibly *USS Texas*

his men for the demonstration that he hoped would put an end to three years of bickering over the importance of air power. In June 1921, reports of race riots in Oklahoma, new releases on Broadway, and congressional wrangling filled the headlines. The most prophetic tests of American national defense were about to take place.

The first official tests began June 20th, 1921. They would last a little over a month, ending on July 21st. The targets that had been towed into position off the Virginia coast were captured military vessels: the cruiser *Frankfurt*, the *U-117*, the destroyer *G-102*, the formidable battleship *Ostfriesland*; and the decommissioned *USS Iowa*. Navy and Army pilots flying a variety of aircraft carried out the bombings.

The DeHavilland DH4 was the first US plane ever built for use in combat. It had seen considerable service in the last war as a pursuit fighter, and general purpose aircraft. The Martin MB-2, was one of America's first twin-engine bombers. Powered by two Liberty 12 engines, the aircraft had a 73 foot wingspan and a 42 foot fuselage. It was equipped with five Lewis guns, a crew of five, and could carry a payload of 2000lb. bombs. Only fifteen MB-2s, of the type used in the test, were ever built.

Mitchell climbing out of a Thomas Morse Scout

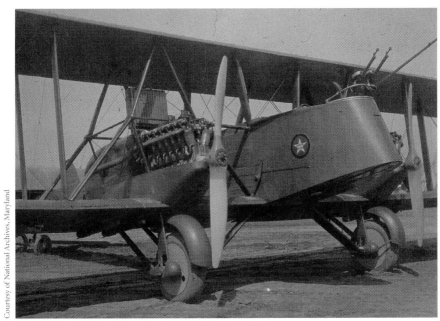

The Martin MB-2 bomber

Among the observers were Secretary of War John Wingate Weeks, General Menoher, Assistant Secretary of the Navy Theodore Roosevelt Jr., General Pershing, and various other international officials, the majority of whom were skeptical regarding the effectiveness of air power. In retrospect, three of the observers set an ominous tone to the occasion. Captain Osami Nagano, who would help plan and execute the attack on Pearl Harbor, took copious notes during the test. G. Shibuta, from the Kobe Chamber of Commerce, and G. Katsuda, from the Japanese House of Peers, were both busy taking pictures of each stage of the bombing, and were particularly fascinated by the timing of the attacks themselves. The entourage of international military representatives and numerous politicians eager to settle the debate once and for all viewed the test from the *Henderson*. As the combined efforts of the Air Service began their bombing runs on the *U-117*, many Naval officers observing the spectacle joked about the planes being as terrifying as moths.

The first hit broadsided the U-boat and the concussion alone had resulted in significant damage below the water line. The second hit caused similar damage. The third bomb hit the coning tower and literally blew the midsection of the *U-117* inside out. The U-boat sank in just under seventeen minutes. The laughter stopped. Mitchell's air tests had begun with stunning success.

The next stage of testing began nine days later under more realistic circumstances. The target was the *USS Iowa*, which was under radio control by a team aboard the *USS Ohio*. The *Iowa* was steaming in an undisclosed location between Cape Henlopen and Cape Hatteras. finding the ship was challenge enough. When she was discovered, the planes scored only two hits out of nearly ninety attempts. This was certainly a setback for Mitchell and the most difficult phase of the test lay ahead.

Two-weeks later, the captured German destroyer *G-102* was the target. DH4s pelted the bow of the destroyer with explosives. The *G-102*, which was one of the only other moving targets during the test, sustained a barrage of simultaneous hits. The bridge erupted in flames and the masts were snapped in half like matchsticks. Within fifteen minutes the ship was listing forward. Just as the bow dipped beneath the surface, the boiler exploded and the *G-102*

Overview of MB-2

sank in under half an hour. Two out of three exercises had met with complete success. Two more remained.

Less than a week later, Martin Bombers targeted the captured cruiser *Frankfurt*. Six hundred-pound bombs exploded beside the ship causing towers of water to swell over the cruiser. The fatal blow came amidships. The explosion opened a large gash down the center of the *Frankfurt*, the ocean poured in and she slowly sank beneath the waves in an almost graceful motion. The sinking of the *Frankfurt* was added to the list of successes for the Air Service, but the greatest test was yet to come. The massive dreadnought, *Ostfriesland*, was a heavily armored battleship. A state-of-the-art war machine made famous during the World War. The vessel was a last hope for those who wished to disprove Mitchell's theories. In 1917, the British navy had called the *Ostfriesland* unsinkable. Now, its reputation would be put to the test.

Bombing began late on the morning of July 19th with minimal damage being done by the pursuit fighters. By early afternoon, a gale blew in and

Mitchell (left) seen standing with Eddie Rickenbacker after the First World War

forced an end to the tests for the day. Anti-air power observers held out hope that the Air Service would be unable to sink the battleship and the years of debate would be decided in favor of the Navy. The next day's bombardment proved them wrong and brought Admirals to tears.

Six Martin bombers closed in on the *Ostfriesland*, and began dropping some of the heaviest ordnance used during the tests. Within fifteen minutes, the once proud battleship was capsizing; the damage done by terrific explosions had rendered the dreadnought a shambles. One blast from a 2,000lb bomb was so forceful, it actually knocked back the cameraman filming it from the air. After witnessing the tests, one of the Japanese observers, Katsuda, was quoted by Daniel Bidwell, of the Hartford *Courant*.

> *Very great experiment, profoundly exciting. Our people will cheer your great Mitchell and, you may be sure, will study his experiments. There is much to learn here.*

When Bidwell questioned Katsuda on the prospect of a war between America and Japan, Katsuda continued.

Courtesy of National Archives, Maryland

Mitchell's DH-4; 'Osprey'

…It would be gravely embarrassing to the American people if the ideas of your honorable General Mitchell were more appreciated in Japan than in the United States. Gratitude is not one of the attributes of democracy.

Despite the stellar success of the tests that proved General Mitchell's theory of aerial bombardment a reality, the military paid little or no attention. An article entitled "The Bombing Tests" published in *The New York Tribune*, describes the seemingly obvious conclusions after watching the ships being blown to pieces from the observation ship, *Henderson*.

A battleship force, however powerful as such, must, when so stripped of support, remain at home! It becomes an impotent factor in naval warfare! …The officers and men of the army and navy aviation forces cannot be too highly praised. They have worked under many handicaps. They have been compelled to fight against conservative influences at the War and Navy departments, as well as in the army and fleet. There

The *Ostfriesland* under bombardment

is fear lest aviation may prove itself too important. ..The aviator has fairly won his place as a factor in war, afloat or ashore. In these navy tests he has only used one weapon-the bomb. He has three others-the mine, the torpedo and gas. ..These facts are astonishingly forgotten or ignored by conservative naval officers and others who insist that anti aircraft can keep off a bombing attack and that a zigzagging fleet can ignore air forces! When the subject is calmly considered the navy will awake to the truth…

The first tests gained notoriety in the national news, but faded almost as quickly as the patience of the politicians in Washington. Assistant Secretary of the Navy Theodore Roosevelt Jr. was quoted using this analogy to describe the tests off Virginia;

"I once saw a man kill a lion in Africa with a 30-30 caliber rifle under certain conditions, but that doesn't mean a 30-30 rifle is a lion gun."

Even in the face of complete success, the Virginia tests were regarded as lucky hits on aging equipment. The politicos, along with the Navy, did

Detail of MB-2

Direct hit on the *Ostfriesland*

Ostfriesland taking a direct hit

everything they could to play down the success of the trials in the media, explaining the *Ostfriesland* was hardly in the shape it had been during the First World War, and its system of 'water-tight' doors were not really water tight. Little did anyone know that it was not just air power that was being put under the test; it was the Nation.

On July 21st, the same day the test off the Virginia Capes ended, the theoretical invasion of the United States was already well underway. Mitchell had created a scenario incorporating the tests on the ships as a part of a much larger exercise. Cape Hatteras was the theoretical beachhead for the landing of enemy troops and where they established an airdrome to stage raids on major American cities.

On the 29th, people in Washington and New York looked skyward to the sound of airplane engines. Mitchell's aircraft flew over both cities to prove their vulnerability to an enemy air attack, and, again, he succeeded. The calculated destruction left the financial district in ruins, city hall destroyed, the capitol in flames, and huge buildings toppled to the ground. Four years passed until the country took notice. *The Washington Herald* in November,1925 published a front-page story with a detailed drawing of a city being destroyed, the headline read; "*This Could Happen-It May Happen*".

Ostfriesland sinking

This picture published in the Sunday edition of W.R. Hearst's Washington Herald, as well as in other newspapers throughout the country, ought to attract the attention of gentleman supposed to be responsible for the defense of the United States. It shows without exaggeration, what would happen to a great city if war, as it is understood today, should break loose upon it. …Imagine an airplane night attack on a city like New York for six millions of people. Bombs dropping in Wall Street, on the Treasury, on the great buildings that tower above the battery would cause some thinking on the part of the high finance and make it wish that it had used its government more intelligently for protection.

Brigadier General Mitchell would be called a traitor to the military by some, a prophet without honor by others, and a true American patriot by the majority of the public. He knew air power could and would make a conflict so devastating and horrible for any enemy, that the thought of war itself would be hateful. His philosophy can be summed up in one word; deterrence. Rather than seeing the airplane as a new opportunity to loose lives, he saw it as a tool to save them, and prevent war from occurring in the first place. How could any Army or Navy on the face of the earth willfully become the aggressor knowing the United States could paralyze their forces within a

Mitchell in France

Mitchell beside racing horse

Courtesy of Library of Congress

few months? Sadly the answer was very simple; prevent that kind of implementation of technology from taking its place within the nation's armed forces all together. Few understood that countries like Japan and Germany were already on the threshold of developing air fleets. Mitchell did understand and, trying to prepare America for a war no one wanted to believe was coming, would cost him his career.

Chapter Four

The Lion Killers

*O*n the Outer Banks of North Carolina, the fight over who controlled air superiority was not a concern on an island controlled by the ocean. Hatteras village was a small fishing community on the shores of a place known by sailors for years as the Graveyard of the Atlantic. Children went to school in their respective villages and, in the winter, a popular treat was home made taffy. Church functions were occasions both spiritual and social for all ages. The people were strong, resourceful and fiercely independent. Hatteras was virtually untouched by the modern world; paved roads did not exist, electricity depended on the weather, and cars were a luxury. Even then, the island possessed a unique identity. It was, and still is, a portrait of American life, captured between sand and sea. Originally, Hatteras had been chosen as the site for the 1921 bombing tests, but the location was changed at the last minute. Now, one of the final chapters in the birth of American Air Power would take place here.

William Mitchell was hardly a stranger to the Outer Banks. He had often gone hunting and fishing on Hatteras as a respite from the almost constant debate with Congress. However, in the autumn of 1923, Mitchell would come to Hatteras not for sport, but for the opportunity to prove his theories conclusively.

Over the past two years, Mitchell had continually embarrassed his superiors through the media. He often ignored the chain of command and went over the heads of immediate superiors to initiate plans of his own or publish stories in newspapers and periodicals without proper clearance or authorization. Mitchell was an egotist, but a necessary one. Regardless of his image as self-proclaimed savior and insubordinate promoter, he was the only one with

Center of Hatteras Village

Austin General Store

the knowledge and expertise needed to implement the air defenses required for the security of the United States.

However, an even more critical event effecting what would become Mitchell's second trial occurred in 1922, when the Washington Naval

The Burrus Grocery (left) and the weather station (right)

Aerial view of Hatteras Village (center) and Hatteras Airdrome (upper right)

Mitchell after a day of duck hunting on Hatteras

Mitchell (left) standing with tuna caught off Hatteras

Limitation Treaty was being negotiated by the heads of the most powerful nations in the world.

> *On the coming into force of the present Treaty, but subject to the following provisions of this Article, all other capital ships, built or building, of the United States, the British Empire and Japan shall be disposed of as prescribed in Chapter II, Part 2.*

Mitchell with pilots   A DeHavilland DH-4

Among the many ships to be decommissioned by the United States were the *USS New Jersey*, and the *USS Virginia*. Naval officials were eager for a rematch with Mitchell and the Air Service and saw a rare opportunity with the two modern battleships. Mitchell was more than willing to show that not only could air power prevail, but it could do what it had done off the Virginia Capes consistently. However, military officials authorizing the test would not make it easy. Throughout the month of July, 1923, Mitchell gathered and organized the bombing section of the Air Service for what he thought would be its final trial. Mitchell kept a typed diary;

July 17th, 1923

Lined up bombing project in the morning.

Completed draft of four letters for General Patrick's signature and a covering memorandum, outlining the bombing maneuvers as I desired them carried out. These letters were approved and forwarded to Langley Field.

Had a chart prepared, showing the training necessary and the time allotted to each phase of it. This was finished up in the afternoon and sent out to be photostated.

Spent most of the afternoon correcting a rough draft copy of my notes on bombardment aviation.

The D-3 airship

Launching weather balloon off Hatteras Airdrome

Cape Hatteras airstrip, Durant Lifesaving Station seen right

Flight officers meeting on Hatteras Airdrome

Mitchell's original proposals requested the *New Jersey* and the *Virginia* be radio controlled as the *USS Iowa* had been two years earlier. He also asked for the use of an experimental 4,000lb bomb called the Mark I, and a radio controlled torpedo in an effort to show the versatility of strategic bombing. The requests were denied. Instead, Mitchell was forced to make use of the old aircraft, along with the left over ordnance from the first bombing tests. In addition, many of his original pilots had left the Service and Mitchell had to race against the clock to establish a stable and well-trained bombing unit.

By the middle of August, Hatteras village had been chosen as the location of the second bombing test. Mitchell wanted to show that a small airstrip located on virtually any coastline in the world could intercept, engage and destroy an enemy fleet. In the process, Hatteras was becoming a depot for tons of construction material, a base for Army engineers and an employment center for local workers. Supplies and labor were needed to help build a major airdrome sixty miles south of Kitty Hawk where the birth of powered flight had occurred only twenty years before. The army engineers were welcomed warmly into the community. Men and boys, six to sixty, came to help work on the airstrip that would be used in the tests. Shanklin Austin, a nine year old, with a cart and shore pony, helped to build the airdrome. He recalled being paid in silver dollars by William Mitchell during the latter's frequent visits to Hatteras to check on the progress of the strip. Despite the stress he was put under by his superiors, Mitchell was constantly flying back

Courtesy of Gary Austin and Family

Martin MB-2 from 96th bombardment group and Mitchell's DH-4 (center) on Hatteras

Courtesy of National Archives, Maryland

MB-2 (center) along with DH4s (rear) on the flight line at Langley Field, Virginia

and forth between Hatteras and Langley. In his diary, Mitchell notes one of his trips down to Hatteras in preparation for the bombings.

August 26, 1923

Flew down to Cape Hatteras in the morning.

Checked up on the progress being made in the preparation of the airdrome.

While there I went fishing and got a great number of beautiful blue fish.

Returned to Langley Field in the late afternoon.

New Jersey

Smoke curtain laid behind the *New Jersey*

Detail of smoke curtain

New Jersey struck by a 1100lb. bomb

Bomb strikes *New Jersey* in stern

New Jersey listing after several direct hits

On September 2nd, he arrived early in the morning, spent the day fishing off shore, and returned to Langley late that afternoon. Mitchell had found a second home on the Outer Banks and a community that would become a second family. Events of international importance began to mingle with the routine of small town life.

As construction neared completion, airmen and aircraft started to arrive on the southern tip of the barrier island. Many people on Hatteras had never seen an airplane or any type of aircraft before; such was the isolation of the community. Carlos Oden, his brother and his cousin were in a boat beneath the bridge that led over Slash Creek one day, when they spotted what looked like a giant silver bomb floating in mid air. The three boys promptly dove out of the boat in alarm and cautiously waited to see where the strange object was going. The 'silver bomb' was a Navy dirigible, which was observing the landing strip from overhead.

The newly arrived pilots had their share of surprises trying to set up an encampment at the airdrome. A steadily blowing ocean breeze combined with shifting sands pitched many of the Army tents end over end. The surf-men of Durant Life Saving Station found the situation somewhat amusing, but offered their station as temporary quarters to the airmen. Weather was a constant inconvenience at the airdrome. Ronald Stowe, who had gathered and sold figs to the airmen by the wagonload, remembered attending the Methodist church in Hatteras village during 1923 when he was a young boy. It was a beautiful Sunday, and the windows were open, when gray clouds appeared on the horizon. Halfway through the sermon, the aviators–having seen the approaching storm–leapt out the windows and doors as quickly as possible, to race and tie down the kite-like aircraft. Half of the airmen reached the strip, while the other half became lost on the island and enlisted locals to guide them back. It was almost September and the pressure on the bombing group, now fully stationed at Hatteras, was starting to mount.

Although Mitchell's requests for 4000lb. bombs and radio controlled torpedoes had been denied, the test would mark two firsts in aviation history. The automatic bombsite, designed by Major Alexander DeServersky, was used for the first time in the bombing tests on the *New Jersey* and the *Virginia*. Bomber pilots during the Second World War would use a similar version of the bombsite with devastating effects on Japan and Germany almost two decades later. The MB2s would also set an altitude record through the use of superchargers, which allowed the aircraft to achieve greater operational heights without the instruments freezing.

A report written by Lieutenant Bissel on September 3rd, outlined the plan of attack.

Two battleships, the "New Jersey" and the "Virginia" are located in the Atlantic ocean approximately sixteen miles east by south of Cape Hatteras light. The "New Jersey" is anchored approximately two miles and the "Virginia" three miles south of the Diamond Shoals Lightship.

Barbecue at Hatteras School for Mitchell

Barbecue at Durant Station

Length of these battleships (overall) four hundred and forty one feet, beam seventy-six feet, and carry two basket masts with three funnels between them.

A destroyer flotilla consisting of five destroyers is stationed at regular intervals on a line drawn directly from the temporary airdrome at Hatteras to the battleships, for patrolling, observation, and rescue purposes.

The board of Air Service observers with officers from the Ordnance Department, Coast Artillery Corps, and Chemical Warfare Service are on the mine planters "John Henry" and "Schofield" stationed in vicinity of battleships.

Mitchell flying DH-4 with command pennant

Virginia

Virginia taking first hit

Additional hits to *Virginia*

Virginia devastated by ordnance

Detail *Virginia*

Virginia sinking

Mitchell at air races

Army and Navy officers, government officials, press representatives and others are on the army transport "San Mihiel" to witness the attacks. This vessel will be stationed at a safe distance from the battleships.

The 19th Airship Company will have the airships D-3 and To-2 remain in observation of targets prior to and during the attack, it will obtain and transmit meteorological data up to an altitude of 6000 feet to the 2nd Bombardment Group and will secure photographs of the attacks and carry on rescue work.

The 2nd and 20th photographic sections will secure photographs of all phases of the attack.

It is assumed that our pursuit aviation has gained temporary superiority of the air and that our attack aviation has successfully completed their attacks at low altitude against the personnel of these battleships.

This group will attack the battleships "New Jersey" and "Virginia" after 8 a.m. 5 Sept., 1923. The northernmost of the two battleships (New Jersey) will be attacked first. This order will go into effect upon notice from the Assistant Chief of the Air Service.

On September 4th, the night before the test, Mitchell arrived on Hatteras to prepare for the bombing trial.

September 4th, 1923

Took off from Langley Field at 7:45 and flew to Hatteras.

The administrative and executive organization of the Bombardment group went to pieces. I had expected this. It was necessary for me to take command of the bombardment exercises and issue detailed instructions in order to insure the success of the bombing.

He spent that evening in the radio shack, relaying messages between Hatteras and Langley, coordinating the next morning's events.

On the morning of September 5th, 1923, the definitive test of air power began. As observers aboard the *San Mihiel* watched, the DeHaviland DH4s and the Martin MB2 bombers of the 96th squadron roared overhead. Officials were certain the ships could not be sunk.

The residents of Hatteras village were less certain the bombing tests would fail. Some worried the ordnance would be mistakenly dropped on Hatteras itself. Indeed, local tradition records that one family was worried enough to board their boat and set out to sea, and only returned to the island after one of the DH4s dropped a 200lb bomb six hundred yards off their bow.

A smoke screen was laid in front of the ships from 2000 feet to block the view of the horizon from the dreadnoughts. The first target to be attacked was the *New Jersey*, an obsolete but still heavily armored Capital Ship. Initially the DeHaviland DH4s dropped phosphorus grenades that caused thick clouds of poisonous gas to rise and envelop the deck and bridge. Following the chemical attack, the MB2s began their bombing runs. The start was inauspicious. The first bombs completely missed the target. The bombardiers quickly made adjustments and a steady stream of hits and explosions above deck inflicted significant damage. Nevertheless, the *New Jersey* remained afloat.

Two weeks earlier the Army had changed the test insisting the bombers drop their payloads at no less than ten thousand feet. It was thought this

Mitchell at air races with modified Thomas Morse Scout

would make sighting in on the ships more difficult. Just as the officials aboard the San Mihiel were breathing a sigh of relief, a 2000lb bomb crashed through the upper deck near the stern of the vessel and detonated against the hull. Ironically, it was the height from which the bombs were dropped that allowed the ordnance to pass through the upper deck and explode within the bowels of the ship. The stern was shattered and air bubbled through the jagged opening caused by the explosion below the waterline. The observers watched in horror as the ship almost immediately began to list to port. The rear basket mast twisted and violently splashed into the ocean as the *New Jersey* slipped onto her side. Watching from his personal plane, the *Osprey*, Mitchell redirected the attack efforts against the *Virginia*.

The sister ship of the *New Jersey*, the *Virginia*, sustained little damage in the opening attacks. However, bombs dropped during the fourth run hit the stern, sending large sections of the deck into the air. As the *New Jersey* sank, the bombing of the *Virginia* became incessant. Like the *New Jersey*, she withstood the attacks, until an 1100lb. bomb smashed into the bow, creating a torrent of shrapnel and debris which literally cleared the deck; taking down both masts, all three smokestacks and destroyed the bridge. Despite this critical damage, the MB2s continued to pound the *Virginia*. Finally, after the stern was literally hollowed out down to the keel, she rolled over and sank.

Roosevelt was wrong. Mitchell and his men had become lion killers. They were able to achieve the impossible in the eyes of the military and do it consistently. Regardless of how brief it was, Mitchell's day of vindication had come.

The reaction from the combined Navy, Army, and political officials aboard the *San Mihiel* was one of bitter disbelief. They charged the representatives of the media aboard an exorbitant amount to use the telegraph, thus only allowing the New York Times to report the story. The other national papers would pick up the news throughout the week. Once again, Mitchell made his superiors look like fools in a very public way. It would be a defining moment; Mitchell had made more enemies than allies.

While politicos in Washington desperately attempted to control the media with regard to reporting the bombing trials, the Hatteras community held a barbecue in the village to celebrate the achievements of Mitchell and his men. Strategic bombing, coastal defense, infantry support; the number of uses for the Air Service seemed limitless. Unfortunately, Mitchell had become so thoroughly associated with the birth of American military air power, that his accomplishments, indeed the very concept of air power itself was ignored by all who disliked him. Nevertheless, the media frenzy that criticized an overly conservative military bureaucracy made the public aware that control of the air was the next dimension to the development of warfare and vitally necessary to the development of national defense. For the moment, Mitchell had won. It would be a pyrrhic victory. Soon, Mitchell's enemies would be given an opportunity to destroy him. The final chapter of Mitchell's career would involve an air disaster, another kind of trial, and a politically inspired military committee to silence him once and for all.

Chapter Five
Death of a Soldier; Birth of a Controversy

On September 2nd, 1925 the airship, USS *Shenandoah* departed Lakehurst, New Jersey bound for Detroit. Its crew of forty-three was commanded by Lieutenant Commander Zachary Lansdowne; a veteran skipper of dirigibles and long time friend of Mitchell. Early on the morning of September 3rd, the *Shenandoah* was caught in a violent storm over Ohio. The airship could not withstand the harsh seventy-mile an hour winds, and was torn into pieces. Lansdowne, as well as fourteen other crewmen were killed immediately. Only twenty-nine of the crew survived. The nation was stunned by the disaster and, in the wake of mourners and Ohio souvenir hunters, the public was looking for someone to blame.

William Mitchell had been demoted to Colonel and reassigned to a post in Texas in a blatant attempt by politicians to silence the advocate of American air defense. More than ever, committees were formed and debates arose over the role of the Air Service. Public opinion was now involved, and it was no longer a topic confined to the halls of Congress.

Upon learning of the *Shenandoah* disaster, Mitchell was saddened by the loss of his friend. He was outraged with the Navy when he learned the accident might have been prevented had accurate meteorological information been available. Overcome by frustration with years of political and military disregard, Mitchell publicly accused Navy officials of treasonable negligence regarding the safety of the crew.

Wreck of the *USS Shenandoah*

The press, Washington, and the entire nation were stunned by the accusations. Many felt he had gone too far and he was placed on trial for insubordination.

A lengthy, complicated trial ensued over the next months. Witnesses including General John Pershing, Major General Douglas MacArthur, and Representative Fiorello LaGuardia were active on both sides of the court martial. The media blitz placed popular support firmly behind Mitchell. Over the last decade, he had continually proved the need for a separate Air Service, and the public viewed him as a patriotic underdog fighting bureaucratic intransigence. Hundreds of pro-Mitchell cartoons, articles, and banners flooded the country. A poem written by Paul McCrea captured the feelings of much of the nation.

> *Oh, Men of Arms, you've grimly shorn*
> *The disobedient eagle;*
> *You've proved that speech by those who scorn*
> *Tradition is illegal;*
> *You've proved that when a soldier slurs*
> *An ancient army custom*

Courtesy of National Archives, Maryland

Mitchell at his court martial

You'll buckle on your swords and spurs
And straightway rise and bust him.

Oh Men at Arms, you've smashed a man;
You tried him, found him sinning-
Now buckle on your swords again
Your fight is just beginning.
No doubt in point of legal fact
You won a just conviction;
But still the public views your act
As martial crucifixion.

You take his rank, his braid of gold
But still the public likes him
His friends increase a hundred fold
With every blow that strikes him.
Oh Men at Arms, this Mitchell row,
You'll find, is just beginning;
Your bad boy is a martyr now-
You'll lose in spite of winning.

Mitchell alongside the Prince of Wales

LEFT TO RIGHT:
Lieut. Gen. Hunter Leggett; Lieut. Gen. Robert L. Bullard; Maj. Gen. J.W. McAndrew; Maj. Gen. J.L. Hines; Maj. Gen. Wm. Mitchell; Brig. Gen. Frank Parker after being presented by Marshall Petain (French Army) with decoration of Commander of the Legion of Honor. G.H.Q.A.B.F. Charment, Hte. Marne. France.

Mitchell understood a finding of guilty was inevitable. He used public attention generated by the trial to promote air power and the need for a separate Air Service that was not attached to the Army or Navy.

The trial ended; he was found guilty and sentenced to forfeit his pay and allowance for five years as well as suspension from rank, duty and command. Mitchell handed in his resignation on February 1st, 1926.

My resignation from the Army, effective today, concludes a service of nearly twenty eight years.

It began as a private in the first Wisconsin Infantry in 1898 and has been followed through the Spanish War with Cuba, the Philippine Insurrection, in Alaska while building the first telegraph lines and opening up the country, in the San Francisco catastrophe, and along the Mexican border. The first wireless telegraph and the first automobiles in our Army were developed in my organization. My travels and

Mitchell inside cockpit of Thomas Morse Scout

studies have included the military and political systems in the nations of Asia and Europe.

Command of our air forces in the World War and the privilege of directing the greatest concentration of allied air power ever participating in actual combat was entrusted to me.

The sinking of the battleships by aircraft projected and completed under my direction has revised and changed all systems of national defense. Hostile navies are no threat to our country if there is adequate air power.

The flights to Alaska and later around the world, the airplane tests across the continent, which led to the establishment of the Air Mail, our methods of fighting in the air and the kinds of aircraft to meet our special American conditions, were also initiated under my direction.

I look back on this record with the greatest pride and with the satisfaction that I have done everything possible for my country. After all these years of service, not one dark spot can be found on my record and not one act which does not rebound to the credit of the United States.

Mitchell with Will Rogers

Mitchell with Will Rogers after flight

Mitchell in retirement

Throughout his retirement in Virginia, with his second wife Elizabeth, Mitchell continued to write essays, publish articles and was a constant advocate for air power. His outspoken nature and strength of character, lasted until his death in 1936.

Ironically, Benjamin Foulois, Mitchell's career adversary from World War One, would eventually take over the position of assistant chief of the Army Air Corps in 1927. Foulois would experience an end to his career that was similar to Mitchell's. Seven years later, after being promoted to Major General and Chief of the Army Air Corps in 1931, Foulois found himself at the center of another public trial of air power. A scandal involving airmail contracts was unearthed and, from February through June of 1934, the Army Air Corps was forced to deliver the airmail. A lack of funding from Congress, in the midst of the great depression, subjected the Army Air Corps planes to harsh weather and overly frequent use. As fatalities sky-rocketed in plane crashes, the media went into an uproar and accused Congress of the same negligence Mitchell charged against the Army in 1926. Desperate to shift attention away from the Roosevelt administration, Congress tried to place blame on Foulois. Over the next year, another stunning public trial would take place and would eventually lead to Foulois's retirement in 1935.

Mitchell's son looking at the statue of his father

Courtesy of National Archives, Maryland

Epilogue

Research is more an art than a science; especially where history is concerned. Some facts are easily proven through meticulous investigation; others remain uncertain regardless of the effort that goes into establishing their validity. In essence, presenting history in a way which is accurate is similar to trying to decide which perspective, on any story, is the furthest from being a lie. Consequently, there will be aspects to the personal and professional journey of William Mitchell, which we will never know. However, it is the lessons that can be derived from his example that are more important.

Ultimately, Billy Mitchell was a man with a vision that could not be appreciated in his own lifetime. He was often vain, brash, and thoroughly undiplomatic. Yet, his ideas were nothing short of genius. Mitchell understood that to maintain peace, we must be prepared for war to the extent that victory is assured.

"The air," Mitchell said, "is the third dimension of warfare." The science and art of war continues to be an ever adapting, ever changing phenomenon in our age. Aerial surveillance, precision guided bombs, airborne operation units and unmanned aircraft have become common place within the last decade.

We can only begin to guess how William Mitchell would view the twenty-first century. One could deduce that he would be both delighted and horrified. It is difficult to understand the meanings of conflict, total warfare and death as they have been understood in the past. Today we are shown a televised vision of war. Weapons systems that do not require a

Bomb crashes into *USS New Jersey*

human component react swiftly and sometimes in error. In some respects, mathematics and science has become more important than leadership. Priorities swing from one extreme to another, often testing the parameters of reason. Historically, it is at these extremes that the greatest uncertainty and danger exist. Once more, national priorities are shifting much as they did on the eve of both world wars. Mitchell's career suggests, that it may be the ability to gauge these shifts in policy and technology that provide the best insight as to where our priorities should lie.

In 2002, the Graveyard of the Atlantic Museum and the Hatteras Island First Flight Centennial Committee asked me to coordinate an exhibit and a special event to commemorate Mitchell's historic 1923 test off Hatteras. As research progressed and new sources of information were discovered, the political and technological complexities which characterized Mitchell's quest for air power became ever more apparent. Typically,

An overview of Hatteras Aerodrome in September, 1923

the most dramatic evidence, long ignored or conveniently forgotten , was uncovered after the exhibit opened and the first edition of this monograph went to press.

As the 80th anniversary of Mitchell's tests off Hatteras approached, I was contacted by Mr. Charles Brown. He had seen the exhibit, and had some information he thought might prove useful. When we met, he offered me a dog-eared folder and told me the story of his father, Roy, and his connection to Brigadier General William Ritchie. The folder contained a letter addressed to Roy Brown from Brigadier General Ritchie, several other papers and four photographs; two of which were previously unknown. General Ritchie's letter addressed a central controversy:

May 25, 1962

Dear Roy,

This is by continuing a discussion we had exactly two years ago. You will recall that I was at Hatteras with Mr. and Mrs. Lucas, Bob

Billy Mitchell after a fishing trip in 1923

Ruley and yourself, fishing the "SIKI". On the way in one day we discussed the bombing tests off Hatteras in the days of Gen. Billie Mitchel(sic). You recalled that they loaded bombs and refueled on the beach there, in fact, that you helped. On the other hand, I had the impression that this had all been done from Langley Field.

I knew that you must be right, since you had been there while I was just a cadet at West Point and had never read the reports of the tests. When I returned to Washington, I set it up as a project to get my hands on the actual report made by the Chief of the Air Service to the War Department. This proved more difficult than I thought as no department seemed to know exactly where the reports were. I finally boiled it down to National Archives and obtained permission to research the Search Rooms of the Air Section. I finally found exactly what I wanted-the actual report on the whole operation with attached photographs.

Not only were your recollections correct, but I also found, in reading associated reports, that the establishment and operation of the temporary forward airdrome were greatly facilitated by the help and

Cape Hatteras Lighthouse   Hatteras Beach

cooperation of the Hatteras inhabitants. This is something to be proud of as this operation was a most important milestone in establishing air power as a versatile and potent factor in the military strength of the United States. Here it was clearly demonstrated that the air arm could operate in lieu of or in coordination with the surface Navy in seeking out and destroying enemy sea power, including the heaviest warships.

You will note, in the photostatic extracts from the report, the fact that the super-charged high-altitude bombers operated only out of Langley Field. I was told about this when I was stationed at Langley in 1940, and this must be where I got the idea that all of the bombers were serviced there.

This further clarifies one of the greatest misconceptions concerning Mitchell's bombing of the *USS New Jersey* and *USS Virginia*. The existence of Hatteras Airdrome and the fact that Martin MB-2 bombers flew from the airdrome is established in chapter four. However, these facts are further substantiated by General Ritchie's facsimiles of pages twelve and thirteen of the official post-action report.

On Saturday September first, an order was received from the Chief of Staff that an attack be made at ten thousand feet and that at least

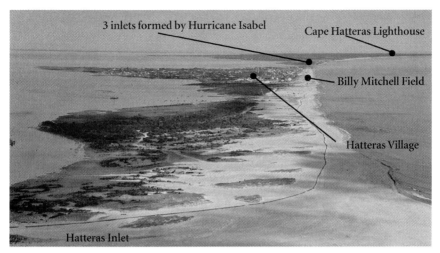

3 inlets formed by Hurricane Isabel

Cape Hatteras Lighthouse

Billy Mitchell Field

Hatteras Village

Hatteras Inlet

Hatteras Island looking west to east

one attack be made at six thousand feet. The attack at ten thousand feet could only be made with super charged ships as an ordinary Martin bomber will not attain this altitude with a full service load. On the date of receipt of this order only one super charged ship was equipped for flights at this altitude. September second was Sunday. September third was Labor Day. The civilian personnel at the shops in Langley Field were available only on September fourth for making the changes required. By working the officer and enlisted personnel from 6A.M. until midnight on Sunday and Labor Day, it was possible to get four ships in commission for work at ten thousand feet. The programme(sic) for the bombing was changed to include attacks at the altitude specified and the personnel flying the super charged ships made one flight to practice bombing at ten thousand feet. A temporary airdrome had been prepared on a sand spit about six miles west of Cape Hatteras. It was inaccessible for any type of seacraft from the ocean side and could only be approached with great difficulty from the Pamlico Sound side.

The water in the Pamlico Sound is very shallow and a barge with a draft of over two feet can not be brought ashore. The landing of motor transport, tractors, drums of gasoline, and 2,000 pound

Martin MB-2 from 96th bombardment group and Mitchell's DH-4 (center) on Hatteras

View looking out of the Radio Shack in Hatteras Village, NC

bombs, was a serious problem under the circumstances. All of this material was successfully landed and moved across the sand to the airdrome. There were no roads suitable for the movement of heavy material.

Weather Station built 1901, photo 1923

Durant Lifesaving Station

Weather Station - restored 2005

Durant Lifesaving Station, three weeks before its destruction at the hands of Hurricane Isabel

A land radio station was established at Cape Hatteras to communicate with planes in the air and with langley(sic) field. An airplane courier service was also provided. Arrangements were made for the

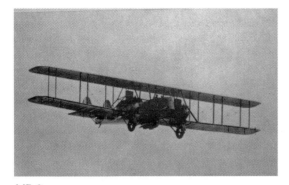

MB-2

Radio Shack

Radio Shack

Cape Hatteras Point

Hatteras Inlet

transporting of personnel in case of injury. The Medical Detachment at langley(sic) Field established a first aid station on the advance airdrome.

The entire bombing group less the flight of supercharged planes flew from langley(sic) Field to the advance airdrome on September fourth. Bombs and fuel had been transported to the airdrome by water. The ships had been refueled and the heavy bombs loaded after the arrival of the Group on September fourth.

On September 18th 2003, hurricane Isabel made landfall on Hatteras Island. It was the most destructive storm to hit the Outer Banks in over a century. Entire sections of Hatteras Village were washed away: motels crumbled and whole buildings vanished. In the course of this storm, Durant Lifesaving Station was literally dashed to pieces. The only extent element of the historic station is a small wooden outbuilding used by Mitchell as the land radio station as described in the report. It survived because, prior to Isabel, the Austin family donated it to the Graveyard of the Atlantic Museum where it is currently on display. We are losing our history at an astonishing rate and, as it fades, we loose a tie to our collective past that allows us to better understand the future.

Hatteras Village

3 inlets formed by Hurricane Isabel

Another view of 3 inlets formed by Hurricane Isabel

The future is hope and a promise of freedom that must, in part, be secured from the air. We all know this lesson too well. Our brothers, sisters, families, and friends in the Armed Forces are called upon time and again to defend freedom in the skies, on land and sea.

Dreams of flight often fade to the harsher realities of war. Despite those realities, there remains a spirit of unfaltering curiosity, which propels us towards a greater knowledge of the world around us. All those share this spirit whose vision leads them down a different path.

Now, largely forgotten by the public who once made him a hero, William Mitchell is continually vindicated by new developments in national defense and aviation. He dedicated his life to the advancement of air power and in service to a country he dearly loved. There is no doubt his visionary understanding continues to inspire both.